INCOGNITO

A COLLECTION OF POETRY
by Giovanni Thompson

ACKNOWLEDGEMENTS

God. The Man Above.
My Family.

TABLE OF WONDERS

INCOGNITO

incognito

i want to vanish from the world
and stay hidden
i'll pass on the polaroids
these are memories i don't want
with someone who hurt me
they broke me
and made me feel like a stray dog
i found a message in a bottle
in the middle of darkness
and it gave me the okay
to hide in the shadows,
f o r e v e r

in all honesty,
i'm a lost boy,
and i don't want to be found

home of a butterfly

you held my heart up to the light
and saw everything inside
you revealed the bruises
i tried to hide from you
i didn't want you to be broken too
with no clue why i happened to you
i'm severely damaged
and my past can't be bandaged
the blood is too much to manage,
but butterflies landed on my heart,
made the vandalized pieces depart,
and turned them into art
the world of healing
was foreign to me,
so a birth in bliss was hard to see
i never knew my heart could be
home to butterflies

<ins>*trial & error*</ins>

i'm well aware of mistakes
that i've made
i failed so many times
with the efforts i gave
endless attempts
for a slap in the face,
so i won't say it's easy
to restart my race
it takes everything to try again
what felt like not having
the courage to continue,
was a being named resilience,
telling me to never change
the sway of my heart
whenever i get knocked out
by the wind

i learned that it's not
about me overcoming,
but *becoming*

the good side

in the midst of your new beginnings,
i'm having a hard time letting go
when you dropped me like a bad habit
and i'm stuck in a timeless phase,
where i'm descending into midnight,
by seeing you happy
with the good side
of what we could never be
so many apologies
i sent out in the air
for writing too many poems about you
i can't move past you,
and what hurts the most
is knowing the constant nostalgia
i feel stems from me
not having the strength to continue,
when my heart's a dying fiasco

so i wish you everything
on your new chapter
because i'm still stuck
on this last one

heart of glass

i give you myself,
vulnerable & honest
i'm open to share,
my heart is my promise
it's heavenly fragile,
embrace it with care
look right through me
& i'll meet you right there
i broke down my walls,
pulled myself out of fetal position,
when i stood my emotions tall,
i saw you as the piece i'm missing
you send all my doubts,
out into the air
so invite me to infinity
& i'll meet you right there
i've been through too much,
and it's hard to get past
but when i found you,
it doesn't feel like
i'm loving too fast
with my heart of glass

silver linings

i never question
if there's a way out
because i have faith
that darkness always
precedes the light

i never wonder
if things will get better
because i know
the sun pushes through
after centuries of rain

i never doubt
if the dark will consume me
because moonlight
still blankets the night
even when the moon
is not whole

roulette

i hope i'm not gambling my life
by putting my trust
in someone else again
in this game of life,
my heart is used to playing
by its own set of rules
and something's telling me
to break them for you
but for some reason,
you don't make me question it
i'd go out on a limb
and close my eyes
and roll the dice
to see if what i'm feeling
is something to pursue
and if my heart doesn't reroute,
then i know it's true

if i show you my deepest secrets
and run to you when i'm sleepless,
would you watch me fall
and crumble on my own?
or trace your fingers
along my weakness
and comfort me where i need it,
so i'm not drowning alone?

i'm just an blank space,
an empty vessel fractured
with no value
waiting to be filled with something

staring at the sun

the dialogue in my head died down
and my nervousness
is sleep and sound
whenever i'm staring at the sun,
happiness and i become one
somehow my body feels alright
when i fade into ultraviolet light
wanting to see the good times
only makes me blind,
but this is the happiness
i've longed to find
it makes me sedate
my sadness in place
and illuminate my heart
in its cage

i catch myself daydreaming,
wondering what it's like to smile
what felicity would
feel like worthwhile
even though all of this
is makeshift,
divide my body on the sunbeam
in the rift
between happiness and my hand
because that's where my heart
wants to stand

S.O.S.

i'm wishing someone sees
my distress signal
to save me from my ship of gloom
i'm fighting things i won't explain
and i can't turn to anyone
even though no one
knows what's happening,
just understand that i'm in danger
it's tiring to continuously
send messages out
when my body's wrapped in morse code
my lungs are filling too quickly
so please come save my soul

is there anyone out there?

the fault in her star

if she has to endure your pain,
then she'll feel eternal ease
within my arms
we are one
i understand how she feels,
although she makes mistakes,
but don't we all?

so, who are you
to judge someone off their faults,
when you were forgiven
for all of yours?

hourglass

it feels like a death
now that you've left
i can't stop thinking
about how connected we were
but then you drifted away from me
and left me solitude on these tracks
i sit here with my heart
that you shattered
can't you see i'm in pain?
it hurts even more
to see you in the arms
of someone else
we weren't lovers,
but we were soulmates,
deeply great friends
i swear everyone thought i had a crush
on you,
but in the end,
the bottom on your feet
crushed on me

INCOGNITO　·　Giovanni Thompson

do you know what it feels
like to be covered in saliva?
i doubt it because you were the one
who spit me out like nasty food
the harder i try to
drive you out of my mind,
the easier it is for me
to speed back to you,
and i crash head-on

every.　　*single.*　　*time.*

i hear the chiming bells
ringing like alarms
the red lights warning me
that the worst is coming
life's telling me
to get off the train tracks
before the train of sorrow kills me
but when it hits,
i'll have no choice
but to flip the hourglass
and relive my crash all over again

save as draft

i'm so used to constantly
rereading our messages
until the point where
it become obsessive
witnessing the falling apart
of something good
is dreadful knowing
i was involved
the further i scroll,
the longer the conversations became
and the closer the connection grew
so to reconcile for the better,
i take deep breaths
then pour my heart into an empty box

erasing every truth
and rewriting every feeling
reminds me to
stop giving olive branches
and to let things
play out as destined

so i save as draft
as some things
are better left unsaid

violet

until memories fade,
and life departs,
you'll live forever in our hearts

we love you.

sync

the echoes of your heartbeat
is the melody my soul sings
i feel at peace when i hear you breathe
i loop that rhythm to help me sleep
all my worries fade away
while i lay in the dark,
syncing to your beating pattern

flare

like a flare in the night sky,
my heart is a beating vessel of light
it guides me through
the tunnel of darkness
and it's insane how
this embedded emblem of hope
in my chest
can pour luminous glows of light
into a world so dark
at times when it's dim
pray to me when you need light
and like a shooting star,
i'll bring that light to your life
as i try to pave my heart a way
while learning the hard way,
i hold on tight to my light
so no one takes my heart away
i'm incredibly fragmented,
but i still manage to put
my pieces together,
to flare when i can,
just like a firefly

weeping willows

i'm stranded, lonely
on a quiet road so coldly
shards of shattered memories
cut my blueberry feet
the eyes of weeping willows
are staring at my heart weighing down

behind me is darkness,
before me is eden
i want to bloom,
but it's not my season
the eyes of weeping willows
guide me with my broken feet

let me show you

there are people who will
lay eyes upon my writings
that never expected me
to harness the power
of painting a world
with only my words

hummingbird

i dream to float free,
where peace and light meet
liberated from the damage that holds me
& free from the sound of heartache
i want to walk through
the field of serenity,
illuminated by the golden hour,
where i bleed the symphony
of the hummingbirds i see
when i breathe

tsunami

i need a cure for these tears
i've been floating
in them for centuries
of life and fears
water pours from my iris,
like a running faucet
i wave back at myself
diving into an ocean of pain,
to help me storm my way,
through life and its fate
all the moments
that i drowned with fear
ripples along the tide of my life
to meet me on this day

it reminds me to swim in the moment,
to take my feet off the shore,
to become one with the water,
and to not stay in the boat,
when i was called to walk on water
i bathe myself
in the sea of forgetfulness
to sail away from the ghost of pain
that flows in the corridors of my life

love & war

you can pour endless amounts
of your all
into someone
for them to one day
run away with it
and choose themselves

in the end,
you cannot be upset
because all is fair
in love & war

distant ones

i miss you
even though i can't remember your voice
your laugh is blind to my mind
it's sad that someone
i once was close to
can feel so far away
and out of arm's reach
it feels like everything
has gone wrong,
but missing you from afar
is right for me
i don't have to mentally beat myself up
to get you out of my head

breathing

hold me tight and never let me go
i find refuge in you
let me fade away in your arms
into a blank space,
a world with love and light,
where only our hearts are breathing
can you imagine a world
where only our hearts are glowing?
whenever i get anxious,
you assure me that everything's okay,
and to just keep breathing

i realize now
that all my anxiety and tears stay at
bay
when i lay my head on your chest
with your heart on speaker

head in the clouds

i turn problems that don't exist
into false realities
i fall into through the midst
of spending hundreds of hours,
wondering if everyone sees and feels
what's wrong with me
they say overthinking can kill you,
but how do you stop a force
that's enabled within you?
my thoughts have a funny way
of never going to bed,
trying to figure out
what would've changed
if i said this
and did that
another way

28

the truth of being black

sometimes i feel like the world gives
me the ultimatum
of bowing down or losing my life
that's like blackmail, right?
but blackmail is illegal
so why do they treat me
like being a black male is illegal?
i can keep a weapon on me if i want to
because this black male is legal
they preach about how
we should pull ourselves
out of poverty
but when i checked my mail
and got that black card,
they said that me receiving
that black mail is illegal

and i'm like damn, am i a pesticide?
having my life unnecessarily raided
like it has a pest inside?
ready to shoot me for anything i say
like they're trying to put a pest aside
everyone oversees what i have
to offer the world,
but they rather ship me
like slaves overseas
all because i keep my grades over C's,
so i'll never try to overseize
the bad things destined for me
and the sad part is,
that's just the truth of being black

i am me.

i'm so used to being held back
by the limits the world places on me
that i neglected the voice
i have of my own

i'm no longer living for anyone else
i'm in control of my own life
and i'm taking it back

runaway

i ran away
from a war only i can stop
from a war that i had
the strength to seize
to save myself
i left you all alone
helpless. scared. frozen.
traumatized. shook. broken.
with your eyes
in the shine of the knife
i was only dreaming,
but it felt surreal
to hear you pleading for help
with my ears piercing to listen,
and my eyes bleeding to witness
i can't lose you
you are my life
you are my heart
i promise that i'll be there
to take a slice
to the heart for you
and cradle you in my arms
for i now know how to move on
and to save you

to infinity

i spent so long
silently searching for the one,
who i felt gave security to my heart
i haven't felt this type
of love before,
and i know my heart is yours to guard
we talked where the water
kissed the sand in hawaii
i remember you asking me
if i were to fall for you,
if i saw us lasting until infinity,
and i said,

"yes, i do."

spilled milk

i stopped crying over spilled milk
and poured myself another glass
because shit happens
when shift happens

life jacket

i need you now
i'm struggling
to keep my head above water
i swam through every ocean to see you
the water that surrounds me
is washing the love i have for you
out of my heart
and filling it with confusion
i tried to go with the flow
of the waves
but the synchronization
of my heart and the wind
pushes me back
when i try to swim closer to you
please convince your heart
to throw mine a life jacket

bite the bullet

you said an angel cried when i died
do you remember running
on your sensitive soles
to my sensitive soul floating away
in hopes to reunite
our sensitive souls?
you tried to step in front of me
and bite the bullet
that had my name engraved on it
you said it's cliché to say
you loved me with all your heart
so you loved me with your soul
hopefully down the road,
our souls can reconnect
so you don't lose me again

moonlight

before you speak,
open up the vessel to your heart
and let mine in
i don't want to witness
the death of a human heart
that's foreign to the love
that shines from the moonlight
glowing in my hands

clementine

i dreamt of paradise
that night i slept
on milk-white clouds,
covered in the sweet
scent of clementine,
beautifully blended with the fantasy
i fueled with you
it's the palace
i never knew i wanted to live in

pain could be falling from the skies,
the world singing along
to the death of my heart,
the butterflies losing their colors,
jars collecting old hearts
like souvenirs

but if i close my eyes,
even in the eye of the hurricane
or on the verge
of losing faith in life,
somehow i can always feel your fingers
lock with mine
and that sweet,
vibrant smell of clementine
tickles my nose

burning sage

i placed my heart on your bed of lies
and paraded around it with burning sage
the smoke feels like i'm being baptized
and i don't want to turn the page
not yet, not so fast
i'm blessed to feel this strange
feeling of happiness,
but i can't let this pain drive pass,
and flick me off like a light switch
you put me in a state of mind
where i couldn't state my mind,
so how could you only
let your heart survive
when you never knew the state of mine?
sometimes i stick novocaine in my veins
to numb the feeling of knowing you
it's revelation to no longer
endure the growing pains
because that's all i ever knew
i've adapted to living
with a bleeding organ
and being used as a container
for your rage
you siphoned what you thought
was important
so, leave me behind
with this burning sage

stuck on you

i wish i could paint the sky
different shades of my heart
and show you why
my love for you is pure as art
i get butterflies when you smile
show me all the shades to love you
learning your hues is bliss worthwhile
keep observing me the way you do
i'm stuck on you

heatwave

the heat signature that your touch
tattoos on my cold face
warms my cheek
the heat signature that your touch
prints on my colorless skin
is like a drop of blood in snow
it hit me like a heatwave
i've never met someone like you

the blacker the berry

i feel the weight of passing feet
and rebellious irises
as i witness white hands
sway past me
and pick sweeter fruit

there they grow,
fruitfully into a divine
spectrum of colors
that signify better days to come,
covered in drool stains
from quivering mouths,
ripe to perfection
in all their glory

and there i am,
watching from a distance
with my thin stem
hanging around my neck,
deeply dark as midnight,
with hints of red from my blood
that drips like tears

the sweeter the juice

they say
"the blacker the berry,
the sweeter the juice",
but if the berry is on the verge
of falling to the ground,
letting go from the world
with scarlet bruises,
how can the fruit be sweet
when it's rotten?

and there i rot
into the same repetitive,
odd black form
they won't want to pick me now
and i don't think they ever will

canvas

i opened my heart to you,
and out poured
a stream of colors and paints,
rich in hue,
and full of life

sad boy hours

i'm slowly dividing from consciousness
the voices in my head sound ominous
they say when it rains, it pours,
but i've been soaking in it
like clogged pores
i'm crying in my heart and it aches
because all i want is to
just erase my mistakes
and stay in a blank state
with a blank slate
no thoughts
just an empty head
where mercy was once sought
nobody knows how thin
i've been stretched
like my vocal cords when i thought
crying for help was far-fetched
i'm alone in the middle of a hurricane
and masking my hurt
is only making me insane
the pain robbed me of my innocence,
but in a sense, i let it happen
i think it's time to fade away
and become mute

pyromania

i lose myself
when i spiral out of control
this inferno heart
that's embedded in my chest
is destined to burn kingdoms
so i pray it rains
to put out the fire
that's cheering
on my burning heart

guardian

you tried to sneak into my heart,
and got caught by my scars
they said, *"no more!"*,
you've damaged me enough

self-inflicted I

you told me it wasn't your fault
that i broke my own heart
i fell for you from the start,
but chasing after you is
when i fell apart

you told me i loved someone
that wasn't there,
that i committed suicide
by falling in love
i died for you to love me
like you care,
but i was all you wished
to get rid of

self-inflicted II

you told me that my love
was my own wrecking ball
and like a pendulum,
it came back to hit me
i built hopes up like a skyscraper
for your call
the taller it got,
the more you branched away
like a tree

you told me my wounds were my impact,
that i took my heart and bruised it
there wasn't any physical contact,
but it felt like
you took it and abused it

compass

i lost the direction of my compass
now i'm feeling kind of homesick
i can't find my balance on the solstice
my heart was warm, now it's the coldest
my soul spilled, so hold still
because i'm tipping off of the axis
in a battle with my mind
when i ask this,
is the temporary stuff a distraction?
or do i take all in like an addict?

shrugged shoulders

i'm terrible at hello's
and great at goodbye's
my life is like an open door,
people walking in and out

welp.

sunset boy

all my doubts sail away
to the rhythm of the sea
where the sky meets the waves
is where i'm destined to be
i rest along the shore with my thoughts
sinking into sweet quicksand
i feel nothing but sereneness
as i see the horizon expand
what a beautiful sunset,
soft to my eyes
hearing birds harmonize
and seeing monarch butterflies
fifty shades of amber,
fifty shades of yellow,
fifty shades of carmine,
with a view so mellow

<u>*who he becomes*</u>

i've taught myself to love
i've taught myself to forgive
learning to forgive those
who damaged my heart
healed me so gracefully
that i witnessed myself grow

i flipped my tragedies
into remedies
for a healthier me

trajectory

i was damaged at the bridge of better
until i crossed it
so i can't wish you the best
when you lost it
i gave you my all,
but you never could recall
i've never felt more broken in my life
it feels like my heart
collapsed on the inside
those nights i couldn't focus
those nights i felt hopeless

there came a time
when i realized
that i deserve better
i never thought i'd ever come this far
from the moment
you fractured my heart
my life set it's track
so what's left for me here?
i made peace
with carrying wounds on my back,
knowing that good intention was there

outcast

you use me to throw me away
it's obvious i'm not wanted
for all the things i've done for you
i'm humble for being generous,
but at least appreciate what i do
act like i'm a part of the conversation
and stop shutting me out
for you to yell at me for being nice,
for being there for you,
for looking out for you,
it hurts
it shows me that my company
is one person too many
it builds a wall
behind you and i
the further you push me out,
the less i'll care
then when you really need someone,
i won't be there

bon appétit

eating away
at our nerves
only swallows us into oblivion
our veins becoming filled with ambrosia
pass me the napkin

shall we feast?

fake smile

wholeheartedly,
i admit i'm falling out of harmony
with my emotions
trying to fake a smile,
but i'm afraid i can't hold it
convincing myself that i can control it
emotions coming down,
falling hard like it's pouring
they see the pain running
through my eyes
and i don't want to cry
if they ask me why
sometimes my fears get the best of me
so writing away memories is my therapy
when it's time for laughs
and joy to fade,
i switch masks because i'm too afraid
failing from within
i wish it never stayed
now i'm shutting off,
shaded by my palisade

lonely road

strolling down a path
with my head bowed
with pain holding my hand
and regret pushing my legs
sonder awakens me
to the distant souls passing by
i hear their voices
whispering a language
that only my mind can decipher
and my pen could understand
i realize that this road
is a getaway from
nightmares
pain
regret
betrayal
tears
and my pen knew how to get there

here i am

it's terrifying how much hate
they harbor within,
all because they fear
the color of my skin
in the midst of our pain & suffering,
here i am, standing in my melanin
i won't stay silent anymore
there's nothing left in me
but to wage war
and there's too many tears
for me to ignore
for black lives to matter _too_
is all we ask for
i heard the pain in his voice
when he couldn't breathe,
clenched purses when i walk
down the street,
the mercy my brothers on trial plead,
and on black people
they continue to feed
they want us to buy their can of bull
so they can feed on us like a cannibal
and shoot us like a cannonball

INCOGNITO · Giovanni Thompson

we've had enough
at the bottom of the totem pole
so we're raging in the streets,
steaming like a sewer hole,
filled with anger
for the innocent lives they stole
to update their agenda
with new death tolls
rest in power
to those taken by the hands of police
forever i will fight,
forever i will stand
so if i have to be ripped apart
to put the world together,
then lay me on the front line
and pull the trigger
here i am

unforgiven

what is vision when you're blinded
by your regrets?
timelessly trying to move on,
but scared to take the next step,
knowing your past will greet you there
they say life's too short
to think about the past
and that everyone makes mistakes,
but why do i constantly feel
like i'm redeeming myself
over and over and over again?
it's like i'm stuck in a cycle
where if i take one step forward,
i take a million steps back

the heart upstairs

there i layed,
chained with my eyes
on the cracked ceiling
for nights at a time, i prayed
for my heart to start healing
it's locked up in the heavens
for angels to cry over it
i try to keep the dead essence,
but it refused to submit
my heart dripped blood on my forehead
like chinese water torture
i couldn't move out of the bed
because the burning sensation of my
heart being gone
makes my soul dry like it's a scorcher
i never knew my heart
could walk upstairs
and leave me down here all alone
with my list of repairs,
ready to be reset in stone
everyone would've thought i was crying
the way the blood of my heart
raced down my face like hopeful tears
my soul feels like it's dying
and i can't heal it from downstairs

for the better

we can't blossom
in the same place
that our roots got damaged
we need to embrace
the changing seasons
and not overstay our welcome
until we become
dead leaves on a tree

sooner or later,
we have to let go to grow

i promise we'll be okay

erase

you saw the levels
of my heart slowly decline
so you came into my life
to try to heal what was left of me
and i shut you out
every time you come close,
i back away
just feeling the body heat
of someone in close proximity
traumatizes me so badly
that i shake uncontrollably
i don't want to know what love is
because what i knew love to be
was having my heart sliced by words,
my head bloodily punched into,
being beaten until i couldn't see,
and forced under water
whenever i made a mistake
so if that's what love is,
then shoot me before i ever
get to feel it
and write love on the bullet
so everyone knows it was
the last thing i felt

that type of love was
never on standstill
yet, i still couldn't stand them
for not hurting me
because that's all i'm used to
melatonin doesn't help me
sleep at night
knowing my life could be gone
at the speed of light
every time i close my eyes,
i feel every hit,
every gash,
every slice,
… every mistake
please just leave me here in the quiet,
and let me drift into nothing

dear diary

waves of emotions
poured in the diary
you're making me out of
you close the book
every time you get your feelings out
and never worry about my own
i can't count how many times
everyone tattooed their stories
over mine

chained to my pen

a voice of an instrument that
understands the rhythm of my emotions
moves my hands a million miles a minute
when crisis lies in my iris
tattooed in the palm of my hands when
adrenaline bleeds into my veins
drowns my paper with sorrow
tearing me apart
i'm chained to my pen like shackles

shackled, i'm chained to my pen
i tear apart with sorrow
drowning my paper
adrenaline bleeds into my veins with my
pen tattooed in my palms
the crisis that lies in my iris causes
my hands to move
a million miles a minute
it understands the rhythm of my
emotions like a voice to an instrument

when happiness is home

have you ever woken up
and felt alright?
nothing was wrong,
it's like you just feel fine
when happiness is home,
accompanied by the light,
i feel grateful to be here
and happy to be alive

<u>starlight</u>

there's nothing i want more
than to look where the stars sleep
and bare witness to them aligning
in the ways we never could
so as the night steady grows,
and the skies glisten,
i hope i see a shooting star
to send my wish up in the air
of possibly realigning ours

gone with the wind

you floated away from me
like a balloon lost in the wind
and i'm still hanging
onto that string of happiness
you inflated me with
i feel like a broken child,
lost with no hope
my heart deflated like a dying balloon
please float back to me

boy meets world

i promised the universe
i'd give my light
even though i've been left in the dark
that felt like centuries
with empty sight
i was left in a box like a check mark
broken promises were the only
words i drank
out of a cup of lies
that drowned me in a tank
that are full of tears like goodbyes
i gave portions of my heart away
with the strain in my poor shins
the crocodile tears i fell for
flooded the way
of my clear vision,
but my heart is huge
so, i try to test the world
one heart at a time

caged bird

there will soon come a day
when you'll need to choose
between staying solitude in your cage
and soaring high like a canary
because there are worlds inside you
that are waiting to be explored

orbit

i could travel light years
through the endless universe,
and just like looking at the sun
on a highway drive,
your energy follows me wherever i go

though our chapter concluded,
we promised to give each other space
before we let ourselves fall
into the black hole
of never seeing eye to eye
until we stopped speaking,
but my soul is synced
with the universe,
so it's easy to feel yours
wandering out there alone

i'm constantly wondering why
our memories rotate like
the rings of saturn
i sense your aura coming full circle
so when i look to the sky,
i know i'll find you there
waiting for me
because you'll always be
in my orbit

every

every storm has calmness
in the middle of it
every crime has a story
behind it
every hand has blood
on it
every story has a purpose
to it
every death has peace
after it
every happiness has sadness
within it
every painting has broken pieces
underneath it

seeing red

sometimes i don't know how to tame my
anger. my mindset is so damaged that i
don't know how to react accordingly to
a situation when my beliefs, character,
and morals are tested, questioned, and
put on the line. the only person that
gets hurt in the end is me. i regret
every word i said out of anger. please
forgive me. i'm sorry. i don't
genuinely mean to cause any harm. i
take full responsibility of my actions
because i am human and honest enough to
own up to my mistakes to then learn
from them. i'm working on a better,
evolved me. just give me time.

true colors

they say pain
is a consequence of love
i learned the hard way
that when a toxic person
can no longer control you,
they'll control how others view you
the misinformation will feel unfair,
but i rise above it,
trusting that other people
will eventually see their true colors
just like i did

fingerprints on my scars

these fingerprints on my scars
bleed like a fresh wound
i tried to test the deep waters
of opening my trust,
but i drowned every time
now i just have cold feet
if my pain was a person,
nobody could fathom
how many funerals
could be repeated
for one person

my heart is just a timer
counting down to my death

dirt & oil

life in the 1700s was rough for a
nigger like myself
yardwork every hour in hot climate
with hills so steep, i had to climb it
this time around, migration had
mississippi dead
i remember asking master for a capful
of water

"if he miss a sip, he dead!"

*"drink you son of a bitch! you's a boy!
learn how to be a man boy!"*

a nigger was dehydrated from the field
not only was i dying of thirst,
master had a gun to my head
like russian roulette,
rushing me to take the haystack
and roll it
sleeping in sheds like an animal,
polishing wooden floors
i couldn't walk upon
taking care of the field
with no energy,
with countless chores i couldn't count
on my stressed, ashy fingers

INCOGNITO • Giovanni Thompson

but nobody could see it
because it was so dark
that it blended in with my skin
and i was picking cotton
in my dirty overalls
i couldn't get caught in
but overall, i wanted to
boycott this town
i didn't want to get thrown about
like an animal
but i knew that if i said anything
against master's rules,
i'd have a bullet in my head
with my name written on it

all i was ever called
was a dirty nigger
with no hope for a better life

twin flame

i try to convince myself
that if i never got closure,
to keep chasing after it
it's getting impossible for me
to hold my composure
when i know i did nothing wrong
for us to split
i hoped all of this wasn't real
because ties being cut
was not my choice
time passed with no response
from which i could heal
so i'd be lying if i said
i don't miss your voice

every day i breathe,
i reminisce on the sweet
memories we shared,
but what's the point in stopping them
from going sour,
when you never even cared?
i'll never patch up the truth
that the thought of you is my weakness
because you are my happiness
like kids loose on concrete

INCOGNITO · Giovanni Thompson

i saw you in my dream,
where reality was seamless,
a world where i felt a heartbeat
from your dead body
that's engraved in my mind
they say a dream can turn
into a nightmare,
but i felt a pulse in our connection
that i never could find

i felt **you** again
and all life's gifts couldn't compare
to the feeling of having
that void filled
my home is in the glare
of my heart finally shining
in the place it was killed
born from the wreckage with little air

so, i guess it's safe to say that
silence is the closure you need
even though sometimes i cry
and my heart may continue to bleed,
i have to wave
this pain goodbye

glow stick

you may have your heart tampered with,
your worth stepped on,
your feelings dismissed,
your dignity gone,
your voice crushed,
and think it's all over

just know that glow sticks
have to be broken
for the light to illuminate

i'm just overwhelmed!

this noise rattling in my head
is like standing in the middle
of a hurricane,
trying to stay grounded
while chaos rips
everything around you
and i just want to scream
because it's about time
i empty what i've been
continually taking in
day after day
i try to find solace
in a medium to breathe,
but just like birds that migrate,
i'm always finding somewhere
to hibernate in peace

i'm just **overwhelmed!**
and i need a break

85

life goes on

as time progresses,
people change
like leaves that fall
from shallow branches
to the autumn floor
as the days fly by,
i grow fond
that life always goes on
just like water
everflowing in streams
of passing experiences
i don't want
to be stuck
like rocks underwater
while life passes me by
every second
of every hour
of every day
and here you are again,
lingering at the doorstep
in my mind

so who's the say,
you haven't changed too?

not worth my energy

i used to trip
over shit i could've
stepped over
but now,
i'm stepping over shit
i used to
trip on

north star

sometimes my soul
loses sight of where
it needs to go
and wanders through
my darkest of skies
to hide
and stray away
from the light

until i found you
illuminating the thousands
of constellations i had
buried beneath my heart
you guide me
through my dull nights
as you burn brighter
than the light i couldn't see
inside of me

so wherever you are,
near or far,
i know i can always
call upon the stars above
to find my way back home

what's past is prologue

who would've thought
these bandages etched
across his skin
from wounds of his past
would be his shield
and transform him
into a beautiful cocoon
that soulfully wraps him
in preparation for
the monarch butterfly
he is yet to become
he once found refuge
in the destroyed places
where tornados ran wild,
learning to live
within the calm before the storm,
ready to embrace
all that's destined
to follow in his trajectory

though it took some time
for him to be
the breathing source
of his own love,
because his insecurities
endlessly weighs him down,
he began refining
those cracked pieces
written across his heart

and soon enough,
he became able
to be okay with knowing
he is all that he was
and all that he's bound to be

heartstrings

if i were
to ever lose you,
there wouldn't be enough
heartstrings in the world
to keep my heart
from falling deeper
to the darkness
within me
and becoming unable
to be discovered

willful blindness

looking back,
i see how clueless
i can be
and i catch myself
searching for a needle
buried in a haystack
to find a rose
in the midst of beauty,
guarded by thorns
that warn me
to stay away
sometimes i can be
willfully blind
to the things that cut me
i siphon cautions from my vision
and fill it with infatuation
and for some reason,
i do it all the time

love yourself.

our insecurities
are birthed from
standards that we place
on ourselves
by emulating the fruits
of someone else's tree
we pick ourselves apart
instead of loving us deeply
and for who we are
so you can't expect
be loved whole
when you can't
even love your half
our insecurities
can create an abundance
of feral kids
that run free
throughout our lives
and you lose all control
of them the moment
you hate what you see
in the mirror

love yourself.

cloudburst

he finds solace
amongst the clouds
and leaves footprints
all over the sky
as he dances through
the everlasting downpour
knowing that he
once withstood
heavier rainstorms

quiet room

the tranquil that emits
from the silent sounds
of our hushed voices
are the echoes of
our connecting hearts
they speak thousands of words
our mouths can't comprehend
i want nothing
but to let the noise seep
through the shallow cracks
of our growing hearts
and savor the moment
as we sit in silence,
listening to our hearts talk
in this quiet room

lost soldier

ever since i lost you,
everything i see and breathe on
reminds me of the thought of you
and this beautiful sculpture
is molded in all the ways
you shined in me
every day,
i pray for a signal
for you to resurface
and embrace the doors
of my life again
this sculpture
in the middle of a dead road
reminds me that
you're still here with me
even when you're gone

and i'll always remember you
even when this life
fades like you did

metamorphosis

i dedicate this to you
as a tribute for all you lost
and a reward for all you gave

i'm proud of you
for not being afraid
of allowing the art of vulnerability
to dictate where the source of light
beaming from your chest goes

you've found a safe haven
in this world of words
where you escape this reality
that pressures you
into being what everyone wants
instead of just being
you

despite what they've said,
you proved them wrong
by not letting your ego
crumble under the pressure
they've tried to place on you
your whole life
although it got to you sometimes,
you never let it consume you
and turn you
into what makes them comfortable

you have a heart of gold
no matter how many times
you've been done wrong,
you still love
like your pain
doesn't exist

through the storms,
you **persevered**
you managed to
start new days
with the broken pieces
that weren't mended
from the previous ones

you're a living testimony
and breathing pinnacle
of transforming into
someone **better**
someone **stronger**
something **greater**
and you've earned your wings

i applaud the journey
of healing you've embarked on
promise me you'll never
lose sight of yourself
and who you are
because they will always put
a question mark
next to your name

in all honesty,
you're a lost boy,
and i think
you're ready to be found

- incognito